LIVING LANGUAGE®

Learn Italian Together

+ +

AN ACTIVITY KIT FOR KIDS AND GROWN-UPS

Activities by
Marie-Claire Antoine

Italian by
Tiziana Serafini

Edited by
Helga Schier, Ph.D.

LIVING LANGUAGE®, A RANDOM HOUSE COMPANY

NEW YORK

Living Language® publications are available at special discounts for bulk purchases for sales promotions or premiums, as well as for fund-raising or educational use. Special editions can be created in large quantities for special needs. For more information, write to Special Sales Manager, Living Language, 201 East 50th Street, New York NY 10022.

Published by Living Language®, A Random House Company, 201 East 50th Street, New York, New York 10022.
Member of the Crown Publishing Group.

Random House, Inc. New York, Toronto, London, Sydney, Auckland
www.livinglanguage.com

Living Language is a registered trademark of Random House, Inc.

Printed in the United States of America

Design by Jesse Cohen

Library of Congress Cataloging-in-Publication Data

Antoine, Marie-Claire.
   Learn Italian together : an activity kit for kids and grown-ups / activities by Marie-Claire Antoine ; Italian by
Tiziana Serafini ; edited by Helga Schier.
   1. Italian language—Study and teaching (Primary)—English speakers—Activity programs.
2. Creative activities and seat work. I. Serafini, Tiziana. II. Schier, Helga. III. Title. IV. Series.
PC1066.A67   1999
458.2'421—dc21   99-13163

ISBN 0-609-60211-X
10 9 8 7 6 5 4 3 2 1
First Edition

Contents

Introduction   5

Activities   7

Appendixes   40

Introduction

Living Language® Learn Italian Together is a fun and effective activity kit for kids and grown-ups that teaches essential Italian vocabulary and phrases through sixteen exciting, childproof, and easy-to-prepare indoor activities. Whether you already speak Italian and want to teach your children or you want to learn along with them, whether you're a parent looking for at-home edutainment or a teacher looking for additional classroom activities, this program offers great educational fun and entertainment for kids and grown-ups alike. In "Home Planets" your kids will learn the rooms of the house, in "Dice Man" they'll learn how to count, in "Find the Rainbow" they'll learn the colors, and in "Let's Find a Disguise" they'll learn the names for basic clothing items—all in Italian!

The complete **Learn Italian Together** package includes this 48-page book, one 60-minute cassette, and a full page of color play-and-learn stickers.

The book comes complete with a step-by-step description of all sixteen activities, a two-way glossary, and a translation of all songs and rhymes used on the recordings. At the beginning of each activity, carefully read the instructions and gather all the materials necessary to complete the activity. During the activity, follow the step-by-step instructions carefully. Turn on the tape to listen to the two narrators, as they guide you and your children through singing Italian folk songs, creating a fun Halloween mask, hosting your own TV show, and playing a game of "Simon Says." Without even noticing it, you and your children will learn the most essential Italian words and phrases. Suggestions for adapting and modifying the activity to enhance learning conclude every activity.

The book doubles as a scrapbook that the kids can personalize with drawings, photographs, or the included stickers, to create a record of the completed activities.

The appendixes feature a two-way glossary that will prove to be an invaluable reference tool. In addition to all vocabulary used during the program, the glossary includes several thematic vocabulary lists that go beyond the scope of this program.

The recordings feature vocabulary, phrases, songs, and rhymes. The two narrators, Stefano and Fiammetta, lead you and the children gently through each activity. They will teach the vocabulary and phrases and provide ample opportunity for you to practice your pronunciation. Just listen and repeat, and soon you'll be speaking Italian on your own. Italian songs and rhymes help with learning. Don't worry if it seems difficult to follow the songs the first time around. Just rewind and listen to them again. For your convenience, transcriptions and translations of the songs and rhymes are included in the appendix.

And now, let's begin. *Ora cominciamo!*

Activities

Home Planets

Time: 30 minutes

Vocabulary and Phrases: Rooms of the House

la casa house • *la cucina* kitchen • *il salotto* living room • *la sala da pranzo* dining room • *la camera da letto* bedroom • *il bagno* bathroom • *Buongiorno!* Hello! • *(Io) mi chiamo* . . . my name is . . .

YOU NEED ·

✔ **a pen**
✔ **crayons**
✔ **stickers showing a cooking pot, a TV, a pillow, a bottle of bubble bath**

+ +

1. Welcome to **Learn Italian Together.** With this activity kit you'll learn how to say things in Italian, and you'll sing songs and play games. Let's start right away with a game called "Home Planets." In this game, you get to pretend that you're from outer space!

2. Imagine you are an explorer from another planet discovering new worlds! Your mission is to report all you see to the Explorer in Chief, the Great Mirak. The Great Mirak speaks only Italian, so you have to speak Italian, too. Turn on the tape to learn your very first words in Italian.

3. Pretend that each room is a new planet. Land your spaceship in the room and start your report to the Great Mirak. First, say the Italian name of the "room-planet" you're visiting. Then describe what it looks like: How big it is and whether it's populated. If you see people on the planet, describe them, too, and explain what they are doing. For example, if they are on the "living-room planet," say: "They are adults and they watch TV."

4. Travel from "room-planet" to "room-planet" until you have explored the entire system of home planets!

5. Whew! What a great trip you've just made. But wait! The game's not over. Now pick a partner. Pretend you are the Great Mirak and your partner is the explorer. He or she describes a "room-planet" without mentioning its name. You must figure out which "room-planet" he or she is on and give its name. Can you name the room in Italian? Switch roles after you've guessed correctly.

6. Would you like to learn an Italian song about a castle? It's called *Marcondirondirondello* (Marcondirondirondello). Quick, turn on the tape!

7. Look at the house on the right-hand page. Do you know the name of each room in Italian? If you already know how to read and write, write down the name of the room in Italian. If you don't, ask an adult to help you. For each room, find the sticker with a thing you use in that room.

8. Draw your own room in the house on the bottom of the page and color it with crayons.

Home Planets

The Italian House

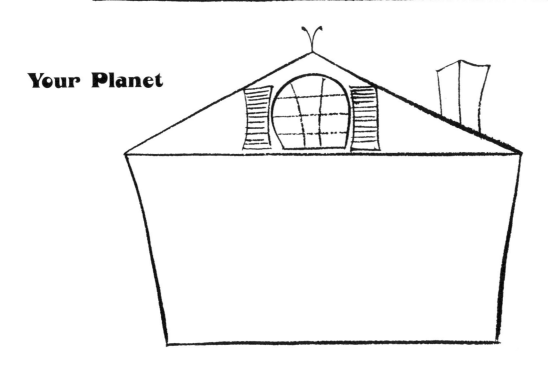

BEDROOM

BATHROOM

LIVING ROOM

KITCHEN

Your Planet

Interior Decorating

Time: 60 minutes

Vocabulary and Phrases: Furniture
i mobili furniture • *il letto* bed • *il tavolo* table • *la scrivania* desk • *la sedia* chair
il divano sofa • *la lampada* lamp • *il comò* chest of drawers

YOU NEED ·

✔ modeling clay
✔ stickers showing a bed, a table, a lamp, a chair
✔ a pen

+ +

1. Today we will furnish your entire house . . . with a little clay and a lot of imagination! Take out your modeling clay and pick a room. Can you say its name in Italian? Good! Now take your clay, go into that room, and start making pieces of furniture for this room. Be creative! Make the furniture you would like to see in this room. For example, if you picked the bedroom, you could make a round bed, a night table shaped like a frog, or a lamp shaped like a mushroom! There are no limits to your imagination.

2. When you're finished with that room, count your score. Each piece of furniture you made is worth 10 points, but if you name it in Italian, it's worth 20 points.

3. Now pick another room. Keep playing until you've furnished the entire house! What's your total score? To get a maximum number of points, turn on the tape and learn the Italian names of some pieces of furniture.

4. To add more of a challenge, ask your parent or your teacher to pick a room and set a time limit. Your parent or teacher will pick the room

you should go to, then give you five minutes to make furniture for it. Count your points the same way. Add a bonus 10 points if you name the room in Italian!

5. If you have a partner, have him or her choose a room. Go into that room and make clay furniture for it. As soon as one player is done, both must stop! Count your score as explained above (10 points for each piece of furniture, 20 points if you say its name in Italian, and a bonus 10 points if you name the room in Italian). Then switch roles so that now you pick the room. Move on until you've covered the entire house. Then tally your total score. The one with the highest number is the winner.

6. Find the answers to the questions on the right-hand page on the sticker page. Put the sticker with the piece of furniture that answers each question next to it. Can you write its name in Italian?

7. Imagine you are redecorating your bedroom. See the roll of white wallpaper? Draw the pattern you would choose for your room.

    10

Sticky Furniture

Where do you sleep?

Where do you eat?

What do you use to
have light at night?

Where do you sit
when you eat dinner?

Fancy Fun Wallpaper

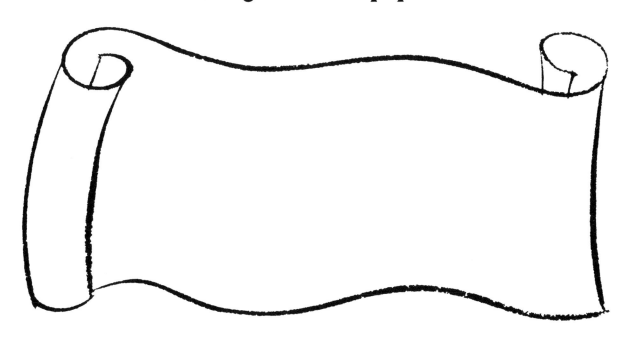

Ace Inthehouse, Detective

Time: 60 minutes

Vocabulary and Phrases: Weather Expressions

sì yes • *no* no • *piove* it's raining • *fa bel tempo* it's nice weather • *fa caldo* it's hot (weather)
nevica it's snowing • *fa freddo* it's cold (weather) • *fuoco* it's hot (game expression)
fuochino it's nice weather (game expression)

YOU NEED ·

✔ a pen

· ·

1. In this activity, you can be a detective and find a hidden object, or be a wizard and guide the detective on his search. Does that sound like fun?

2. You are Ace Inthehouse, a private detective. Your partner is the Weather Wizard. First, you, Ace, must pick a room in which you will play. Give the Wizard the name of the room you picked in Italian just as you learned in "Home Planets." The Wizard will go into that room alone. If you are both already in the room, you, Ace Inthehouse, must leave! The Wizard will hide an object of his or her choice. Then he or she will call you back into the room.

3. Once you're back in the room, start looking for the hidden object. The Weather Wizard will use weather expressions to guide you. For example, if the Wizard says "It's hot," it means you are near the object. If the Wizard says "It's cold," you are moving away from it. To make the game more challenging, the Wizard will speak only Italian! Turn on the tape now so you can learn some weather expressions in Italian!

4. Ready? Here's the list of clues and what they mean. At times you will find two words: the first one is for the weather, the second one is specifically for this game.

5. Go ahead and start playing! When you find what

Weather expressions	Game expressions	
Fa caldo.	*Fuoco!*	It's hot.
	(means Ace is next to the object)	
Fa bel tempo.	*Fuochino!*	It's nice weather.
	(means Ace is near the object)	
Piove.		It's raining.
	(means Ace is walking toward the object)	
Fa freddo.		It's cold.
	(means Ace is walking away from the object)	
Nevica.		It's snowing.
	(means Ace is nowhere near the object)	

you think is the object, show it to your partner. Your partner will tell you if that's the right object or not. If it's not, keep playing! If it is, switch roles and pick another room of the house.

6. Did you like the game? Are you tired? Turn on the tape again to learn a little Italian song while you rest. It's called *Cu-cù, cu-cù* (Cuckoo, Cuckoo), and it's about a cuckoo greeting the spring.

7. There's more fun on the right-hand page! See the drawings? If you use the object in the sun, draw a sun 🌞 next to it. If you use the object in the rain, draw a rain cloud ☁.

8. Finally, draw a snowman. Don't forget to give it a hat and a nose!

or

Mr. Snowman

Circle of Friends

Time: 60 minutes

Vocabulary and Phrases: Verbs

(io) canto I sing • *(io) salto* I jump • *(io) ballo* I dance • *(io) cammino* I walk
(io) mi giro I turn • *(io) rido* I laugh • *(io) piango* I cry • *nel* in the

YOU NEED ···

✔ **a pen**
✔ **crayons**

··

1. In this fun activity, you will mime different actions until there are too many to remember! Here's how to play. You and your friends sit in a circle on the floor. The first player will start by miming an action. The player can choose the action freely. For example, imagine you pick dancing. Stand up, say "I'm dancing," and take a few dance steps. A tango perhaps? (Just kidding.) Of course, you should say all this in Italian.

2. The next player must copy the player before, and then add a second action: singing, for example. In this case he or she would say "I'm dancing," mime dancing, then say "I'm singing," and sing a few notes. The next player will repeat those two actions and add another. And so on with each player.

3. Keep going from player to player around the circle until someone makes a mistake, like forgetting an action or mixing up the right

sequence of actions. Then start a new game. It's easy, isn't it? And don't forget the challenge of the game: You must speak as much Italian as possible. Turn on the tape to learn the words you'll need.

4. More fun with Italian actions? Why not play a game of "Simon Says" using the words you've just learned. To learn how to play that game, go to the next activity called "Simon Says" and replace the words suggested there with the ones you've just learned.

5. Which animal jumps? Which one walks? In the boxes on the right-hand page, draw one animal that jumps and one that walks.

6. Now take your crayons and color all the animals in the zoo. Do you remember the Italian words to describe what the animals are doing? Why don't you write the English next to them?

Salto! (I jump!)

Cammino! (I walk!)

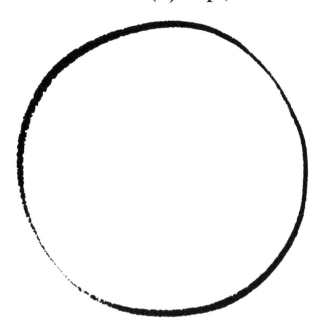 

Zoo Party!

salto

canto

ballo

cammino

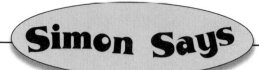

Simon Says

Time: 30 minutes

Vocabulary and Phrases: The Body

la testa head • *il braccio* arm • *la mano* hand • *la gamba* leg • *il piede* foot
il viso face • *il corpo* body • *Stefano ha detto* Simon says

YOU NEED ···

✔ a pen
✔ stickers showing an arm, a foot, a hand

1. Here's an activity that will make you use your entire body. In this version of "Simon Says," you will give orders in Italian. Will your partner obey you? Read on!

2. The game is easy. Give an order to your partner. If you say the Italian phrase for "Simon Says," *Stefano ha detto*, before you give the order, your partner must obey it. If you don't say it, he or she must not move! Another thing: All your orders must ask your partner to do something with a part of the body, like: "wave your hand" or "turn your head."

3. Since this is an Italian game, you must say "Simon says" and the parts of the body in Italian. So quick, *Stefano ha detto* . . . turn on the tape now to learn how!

4. If your partner makes a mistake, he or she is out. If you have several partners, play until there's only one player left. This player then becomes the one to give orders. If you have only one partner, play until he or she makes a mistake, then switch roles.

5. Now give orders using the Italian verbs you learned in the activity called "Circle of Friends." For example: "Simon says: I dance," or "I jump!" How do you say that in Italian?[1]

6. Do you want to sing *La battaglia di Magenta* (The Battle of Magenta), an Italian song about the parts of the body? Turn on the tape again.

7. Uh-oh . . . There's a creature on the right-hand page and it's missing some body parts! Complete its body by adding the stickers showing the missing parts.

8. Now that the creature is complete, connect its body parts so they can work. To do that, match each name in the left column with the part it is attached to in the right column. (For example: the neck is attached to the head). When you're finished, draw the body part next to its name. Can you name some of them in Italian?

Creature

Connect the Creature

This is attached to...   **what?**

nose	leg
hand	face
fingers	head
toes	hand
foot	arm
neck	foot

Dice Man

Time: 45 minutes

Vocabulary and Phrases: Numbers

uno one • *due* two • *tre* three • *quattro* four • *cinque* five • *sei* six
sette seven • *otto* eight • *nove* nine • *dieci* ten • *undici* eleven • *dodici* twelve

YOU NEED

✔ 2 dice
✔ 2 pens
✔ 2 pieces of paper

✔ a calculator
✔ stickers with a die showing 2, a die showing 4

1. Here's a game where you roll the dice to draw a Dice Man! Choose a partner. You each need a pen and a piece of paper. You also need two dice. The point of the game is to be the first one to complete the figure of the Dice Man. The trick is that you must roll the dice to know which part of the Dice Man you can draw!

2. Before you begin, each player must roll the dice once. The player with the highest number starts the game. Then that player rolls the dice again to start the game. The sum of the two dice determines what to draw. If you say the sum in Italian you get another turn! (You only get to roll again once. The next turn is your partner's, even if you said the sum in Italian.) So turn on the tape to learn how to count in Italian!

3. Go ahead: roll the dice! If you get a . . .
   two (2): draw the head
   three (3): don't draw, lose your turn
   four (4): don't draw, lose your turn
   five (5): draw a hand (left or right)
   six (6): draw a leg (left or right)
   seven (7): don't draw, lose your turn

   eight (8): draw a foot (left or right)
   nine (9): don't draw, lose your turn
   ten (10): draw an arm (left or right)
   eleven (11): don't draw, lose your turn
   twelve (12): draw the body

4. If you get a sum for a body part you've already drawn, you also lose your turn, unless you can name that part of the body in Italian. In that case, you get to roll the dice one extra time. (To remember how to say the parts of the body, see the activity called "Simon Says.") Are you ready? Great! Start rolling and drawing!

5. Aren't numbers fun? Look on the right-hand page. Use a calculator to solve each math problem. Write down the result, then turn the calculator upside down and . . . see a secret word appear on the screen!

6. Now break the calculator code! Write the letter each number spells when read upside down on the screen. Can you make up more words with these topsy-turvy numbers?

7. Finally, look at the dice and find the two stickers with the corresponding answers.

Words by Numbers

$$600 + 37 =$$

Secret Word . . .[1]

$$7000 + 334 =$$

_____

$$210 + 7 =$$

_____

$$3700 + 4 =$$

_____

_____

Topsy-Turvy Calculator Code . . .[2]

$0 =$ $1 =$ $2 =$ $3 =$ $4 =$

$5 =$ $6 =$ $7 =$ $8 =$

  [3] =

  =

The Mask

Time: 60 minutes

Vocabulary and Phrases: Facial Features

la maschera mask • *gli occhi* eyes • *il naso* nose • *la bocca* mouth
le orecchie ears • *i capelli* hair • *piccolo* small • *rotondo* round

YOU NEED

✔ three or four white paper plates
✔ glue
✔ scissors

✔ materials to create and decorate masks, such as crayons, paints, aluminum foil, fabric swatches, colored string, ribbons, wool, or felt

1. In "The Mask" you're going to make, well, a mask! First, gather all the materials you need: a couple of white paper plates, scissors (be careful with these; ask an adult for permission and help), crayons and/or paints, a little glue (you'll need an adult's permission and help with this as well).

2. After doing that, search for pieces of string, colored paper, fabric swatches, wool, aluminum foil, pipe cleaners (remember to get an adult's permission and help). You can use anything you think may be interesting to put on your mask.

3. All finished? Good. Now sit at a table and spread these materials in front of you. But before you start making your mask, turn on the tape to learn all about the Italian face!

4. Now you're ready to make your mask. Are you going to make an animal? A superhero? A cartoon character? You decide! Take a paper plate and cut out two holes for the eyes and one hole for the nose. Do you remember what these features are called in Italian? Next, draw, paint, or cut out the mouth, and add the ears. You can glue pieces of paper or fabric to your plate to make ears. Finally, add the hair. Draw it, or glue to your plate pieces of string, tin foil, felt . . . anything you see fit! Use your imagination!

5. As you go along, name each part of the face in Italian. You can also say if each is small or round in Italian, can't you? When you're finished, ask an adult to help you punch two little holes on either side of the mask and tie a string through each. Then put on your mask and play!

6. There's a face looking at you on the right-hand page. But wait! It's missing something! Can you find the stickers that complete the face? Do you remember what these facial features are called in Italian? These four Italian words are hidden in the little puzzle. Look carefully in every direction!

7. Do you have two noses and one ear? Or one nose and two ears? Put a checkmark (✔) in the box that corresponds to the number of facial features you have. To make things more challenging, we've written the features in Italian! After that, draw each feature next to its name.

The Mask

Look at Me!

Face Puzzle

Q	Y	N	A	S	O	C	X
F	R	A	C	C	O	B	Z
O	R	E	C	C	H	I	E
F	K	H	Y	X	A	U	V
L	I	B	E	S	Z	N	A

One or Two?

	one	two
gli occhi	❏	❏
la bocca	❏	❏
le orecchie	❏	❏
il naso	❏	❏

Find the Rainbow

Time: 45 minutes

Vocabulary and Phrases: Colors
il colore color • *rosso* red • *blu* blue • *nero* black
bianco white • *giallo* yellow • *verde* green

YOU NEED +

✔ paper
✔ crayons or colored pencils

+ +

1. On a gray and rainy day only a rainbow will bring color to the sky. Play "Find the Rainbow," and color your day!

2. Take out your colored pencils or crayons. You'll need red, blue, black, white, yellow, and green. Don't worry if you don't have every color. You'll also need some sheets of paper. How will you "Find the Rainbow?" Before we explain, turn on the tape to learn to say the colors in Italian.

3. Okay, now you're ready. We'll play this game in your home. Start the game in your bedroom. Can you name that room in Italian? Great! Now pick one of these colors:

   red (*rosso*)   blue (*blu*)   black (*nero*)
   white (*bianco*)   yellow (*giallo*)   green (*verde*)

   Say its name in Italian, or write it on top of a sheet of paper. Then take a crayon in that color. If you don't have the exact color, take a crayon that has a similar tint (like yellow for white).

4. Now let's play! To "Find the Rainbow," you must look all around the house for ten things in the color you chose. Each time you see some-

thing in that color, draw it and/or write down its name. Once you have ten things on your paper, go back to your room and pick another color, another crayon, and another piece of paper. Look for ten things in that new color. Keep playing until you've gone through the entire list of colors. At the end, you'll have a rainbow . . . of papers!

5. Now play with a partner: one of you picks a color, then you both go look for things in that color. As soon as one player has ten things on his or her paper, the other must stop looking. Count 10 points for each drawing, 20 points for each written name, plus an extra 20 points if you name the color in Italian! The player with the highest score picks another color. Keep playing until you've gone through the entire list of colors. Tally your scores. The player with the highest one wins the title of "Supreme Rainbow Seeker."

6. There's more colorful fun on the right-hand page. First, draw a rainbow in the box. Do you know the color of all the things below the rainbow? Can you write or say the Italian name of the color?

Find the Rainbow

My Rainbow

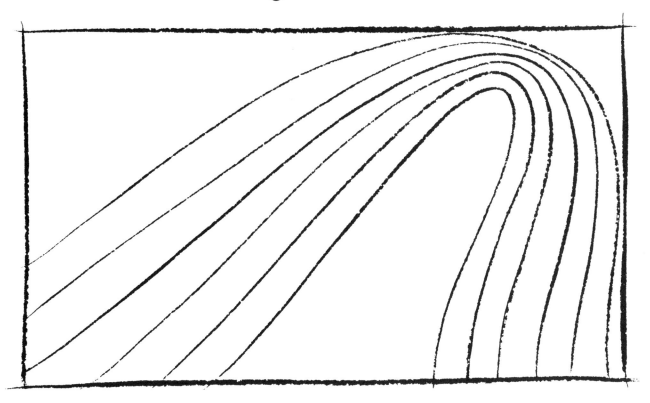

Colors!

The grass is . . .

The sky is . . .

The sun is . . .

A fire truck is . . .

The snow is . . .

Licorice is . . .

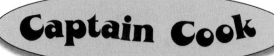

Captain Cook

Time: 30 minutes

Vocabulary and Phrases: Fruits

la mela apple • *la pera* pear • *la banana* banana • *la fragola* strawberry
la pesca peach • *la ciliegia* cherry • *l'uva* grapes • *la macedonia* fruit salad

YOU NEED

For the fruit salad:
- ✔ at least five of these fruits: banana, apple, pear, peach, nectarine, plum, kiwi, apricot, grapes, cherries, pineapple chunks, strawberries
- ✔ a big bowl
- ✔ ¼ cup of water or fruit juice (orange or pineapple)

- ✔ 4 tablespoons of granulated sugar
- ✔ a big spoon
- ✔ a knife

For the game:
- ✔ a pen
- ✔ stickers showing a banana, an apple, a pear, grapes

1. Today you can be the host of your own TV show! You are Captain Cook, the great TV chef, and you are going to explain how to make a great fruit salad.

2. Go into the kitchen and get ready to tape your show. First, with the help of an adult (every big chef has an assistant), put everything you need on the table in front of you. Ready? Wait a second! Like so many famous chefs, you are Italian. So quick, turn on the tape to learn the Italian names of some fruits!

3. Start making your salad. Remember to use as much Italian as possible. Ready? Camera! Action! Carefully wash all the fruits you have. Peel the fruits with a skin you can't eat (like the banana, the orange, the kiwi . . .). Then ask your adult assistant to cut each fruit into bite-size cubes. Put the cubes in the bowl.

4. Mix the water or the fruit juice with the sugar, and pour the mixture over the fruit in the bowl. Stir with a big spoon. Taste. Add some sugar and/or water (or juice) if needed.

5. Now your bowl is full of colorful fruits. Can you name the fruits in Italian? And can you say what color each fruit is in Italian, too?

6. Here's more fun for a chef. Look at the ingredients on the right-hand page. Which ones are used to make a cake? Cross out the ones that don't go in a cake, and circle the ones that do.

7. One more thing: see the empty bowl? Fill it with three stickers representing fruits. Can you say and/or write their Italian names?

Captain Cook

Bake a Cake!

  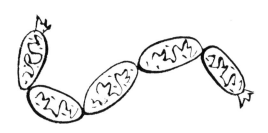

Full of Fruits!

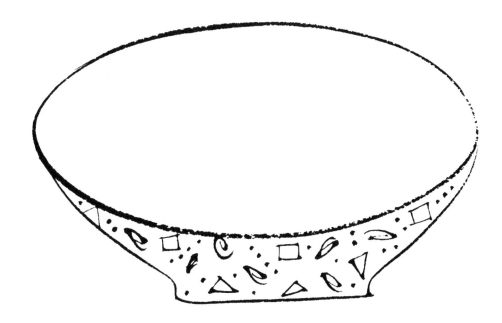

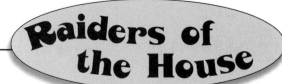

Raiders of the House

Time: 60 minutes

Vocabulary and Phrases: Objects

il tesoro treasure • *il sapone* soap • *lo spazzolino* toothbrush • *i cereali* cereals • *la scodella* bowl
il telecomando remote control • *il pupazzo di peluche* plush toy • *il libro* book • *la palla* ball

YOU NEED +

✔ a pen

+ +

1. In "Raiders of the House" you search the house to find a treasure. The first player to find it is the best "Raider of the House!" Doesn't that sound like fun? It is! So quick, before you start raiding, turn on the tape to learn the Italian names of the things you'll look for.

2. Here's the list of things you must find:
soap (*il sapone*)
a toothbrush (*lo spazzolino*)
cereals (*i cereali*)
a bowl (*la scodella*)
remote control (*il telecomando*)
a book (*il libro*)
a plush toy (*il pupazzo di peluche*)
a ball (*la palla*)

3. Ready? You and your partner must race around the house to find these objects. The game stops when one player collects everything. But wait! There's one more challenge: If you name the object you found in Italian, count 20 points. If you can't, you get no points at all! Name the

room in which you found it in Italian, too, and you get an extra 10 points. Finally, say the color of the treasure in Italian, and add 5 points! Total your points. So even if you haven't found everything, you can still win! You need only speak Italian to be the supreme "Raider of the House."

4. For variation, add more objects to your list (check out the activity called "Forget-Me-Not" for another list of Italian things). You can choose a theme, such as furniture or fruits (look at the activities called "Interior Decorating" and "Captain Cook" to add some Italian words to your list).

5. Are your tired of running around the house? Sit down and look at all those lines on the right-hand page. Follow each one to find each raider's treasure. That done, why don't you draw *your* treasure, your absolute favorite thing, in the box?

sure Mix

My Treasure

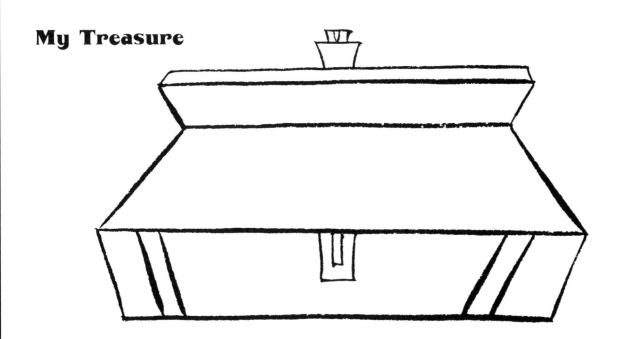

Let's Find a Disguise!

Time: 60 minutes

Vocabulary and Phrases: Clothes

la principessa princess • *il pirata* pirate • *il vestito* dress • *i pantaloni* pants
la camicia shirt • *la giacca* jacket • *la gonna* skirt • *il cappello* hat
lungo, lunga, lunghi long • *corto, corta, corti* short • *(io) sono* . . . I am . . .

YOU NEED

✔ different pieces of clothing to choose from: dresses, pants, shirts, vests, skirts, hats, etc.
✔ aluminum foil (optional)
✔ a big brown bag (optional)
✔ paints or crayons
✔ stickers showing a crown, a firefighter helmet, a plumed hat

1. Look in the mirror. What do you see? Yourself, of course. But can you imagine what you would look like if you were a pirate or a princess? Here's how you find out! First, you need to pick a disguise. Will you be a pirate or a princess? Something else? Choose the disguise you want. Then go to your bedroom with a partner and ask him or her to help you put a costume together.

2. Since you are taking on a new identity, why don't you use your new language as well? Turn on the tape to hear the Italian names of clothes.

3. Are you ready? Use Italian words to ask your partner to give you the clothes you need for your costume. Switch turns once your costume is finished.

4. You can complete your costume with aluminum foil or a large paper bag. Take some foil and shape it into a crown or a sword. If you need to wear something special (like an astronaut suit, or a robot top), you can use a large paper bag. Cut a hole big enough for your head on top, and cut a hole on each side for your arms. Then use your paints or crayons and decorate your outfit!

5. If you want to complete your costume with a mask, you can make one yourself with a paper plate. To learn how, look at the activity called "The Mask."

6. Look! It's Halloween on the right-hand page! See the kids in costume? One is a firefighter, one is a king, the other a great duchess. Only each one is missing something: a hat! Put the sticker with the right hat on each kid's head. When you're finished, color Harlequin's costume.

Let's Find a Disguise!

Hat Tricks

Harlequin

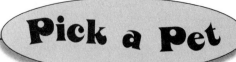

Pick a Pet

Time: 30 minutes

Vocabulary and Phrases: Pets

il gatto cat • *il cane* dog • *l'uccello* bird • *il pesce* fish • *il coniglio* rabbit
il criceto hamster • *la tartaruga* turtle • *l'animale prediletto* pet

YOU NEED ·

✔ a pen
✔ stickers showing a doghouse, a birdcage, a fishbowl

· ·

1. Are pets important in your life? Well, they are important in this game where you pick a pet and mime it. Your partner must guess the pet you are miming and give his or her answer in Italian. Turn on the tape to learn what your favorite pets are called in Italian.

2. Ready? Pick, and mime! If your partner guesses correctly, switch turns. If not, keep miming! Remember: You must answer in Italian.

3. When you're finished playing, turn on the tape again to hear what sounds some animals make in Italian in the song called *Il pollaio* (The Chicken Pen).

4. Pets are good company, so let's stay with them on the right-hand page. Find the sticker that shows where each animal lives and put the sticker next to the animal. Can you say and/or write the Italian names of each animal? Wonderful!

5. Now, read or say the names of each animal. Is it a pet or a wild animal? If it's a pet, draw a little house next to it. If it's a wild animal, draw a tree.

Pick a Pet

Pet Place

Pet or Wild?

tiger

puppy

gorilla

cat

Happy Birthday!

Time: 60 minutes

Vocabulary and Phrases: Birthday Things
il compleanno birthday • *il biglietto d'auguri* card • *la sorpresa* surprise
il regalo gift • *la torta* cake • *la candela* candle • *Buon compleanno!* Happy birthday!
grazie thank you • *(io) ho . . . anni* I am . . . years old

YOU NEED ·

✔ a card-size piece of white cardboard or stiff drawing paper
✔ several old magazines
✔ crayons or paints
✔ scissors
✔ glue
✔ a sticker showing 4 candles; stickers reading *buon* and *compleanno*

· ·

1. Is someone you love having a birthday soon? Perhaps *you* are. In this activity, you'll make a birthday card with an Italian twist.

2. Your Italian birthday card is a collage of different things that have to do with birthdays. Before you start, turn on the tape to learn what these things are.

3. Ready? Good! Then let's prepare your material. You need a card-size piece of white cardboard or stiff drawing paper. You also need various old magazines, crayons or paints, glue, and scissors. Remember: You must ask an adult for permission to use the glue and the scissors.

4. Now look in the magazines for pictures of things you use when you celebrate a birthday. Ask an adult to help you cut out pictures of a card, a cake, presents, birthday candles, flowers,

chocolates, etc. Arrange them on your blank card. Move them around to see what looks best. Ask an adult to help you glue these pictures in place. Wait for the card to dry.

5. Once the card is dry, take your crayons or paints and write "Happy Birthday" in Italian on your card. You can also write the Italian names of some of the things pictured on your card.

6. Of course a birthday is not a birthday without the special birthday song. Turn on the tape to sing *Tanti auguri*—that's "Happy Birthday" in Italian.

7. There's more celebration on the right-hand page. Can you find the stickers that complete the birthday cake? You need candles and the Italian words for "Happy Birthday." When you're finished, color the cake.

Happy Birthday!

Make a Cake

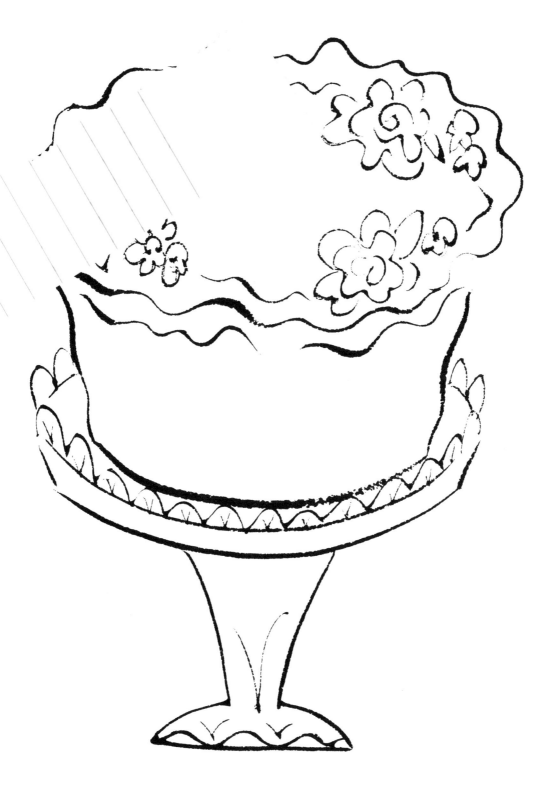

Forget-Me-Not

Time: 30 minutes

Vocabulary and Phrases: More Objects

il biscotto cookie • *l'orologio* watch • *la foto* photograph
la cassetta cassette tape • *la penna* pen • *la spazzola* hairbrush • *il dado* die

YOU NEED ···

✔ a tray
✔ a towel
✔ a pen
✔ stickers with the words *l'orologio, il dado, la cassetta, la penna, la foto*

1. Let's play "Forget-Me-Not" and improve your memory! In this game, your partner will have to remember the objects you put on a tray. So pick a partner, then get a tray and a towel. But first turn on the tape to learn the Italian words that will earn you more points.

2. Ready? Put the following objects on the tray: cookie(s), hairbrush(es), watch(es), pen(s), photograph(s), die (dice), cassette tape(s). One object can appear more than once. For example, you can put two dice or three pens on the tray. Show the tray to your partner and count to ten. Can you do that in Italian? Go back to the activity called "Dice Man" for help. Then cover the tray with the towel and ask your partner what was on it.

3. Count 10 points for each object your partner remembers correctly and 20 points if he or she names it in Italian. Here's a super Italian bonus: count 5 points each time your partner gives the correct number of a particular object in Italian (such as *tre biscotti* for three cookies), and 5 points each time he or she names the color of an object in Italian (such as a *penna rossa* for a red pen).

4. Switch turns. Your partner keeps the same objects on the tray, but varies them. For example, he or she may put two blue pens instead of one red pen on the tray. Or one die instead of two dice. Play as described. At the end of your turn, compare your scores. Who wins? The one with the highest score, of course!

5. If you want to keep on playing, change the objects on the tray. Put toothbrush(es), hat(s), remote control(s), birthday card(s), apple(s), plush toy(s), bowl(s). Look throughout this book to remember what these objects are called in Italian.

6. For each object on the right-hand page, find the sticker with its Italian name and put it next to the object. Once you're finished, draw the face of the watch you would love to have. Don't forget to put in the numbers! Can you say them in Italian?

Forget-Me-Not

Call Me!

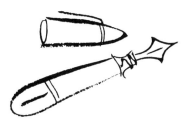 

 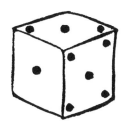

Time to Watch

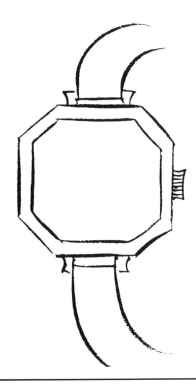

Water Beast

Time: 45 minutes

Vocabulary and Phrases: Animals That Like Water
lo squalo shark • *la balena* whale • *il delfino* dolphin • *il coccodrillo* crocodile
l'anatra duck • *la rana* frog • *cattivo* mean • *gentile* nice

YOU NEED ++

✔ a pen
✔ stickers showing a crocodile, a duck, a shark, a whale, a dolphin

+++

1. Pretend you are an animal as you play "Water Beast." Since this is a game about water animals, why not play in the bathroom? Do you remember how to say bathroom in Italian? Go there with your partner. To play, you need to know the Italian names of some animals that like water, so turn on the tape.

2. Pick one of these animals: fish, turtle, crocodile, dolphin, duck, whale, frog, shark. Then say: "If I were a Water Beast, I would . . ." and describe two things you would do, such as what you would eat, or where you would live. Your partner must guess which animal you are talking about and give the answer in Italian. As an extra clue, add in Italian if this animal is mean or nice.

3. If your partner guesses correctly, switch turns. If not, add another description, and another, and another . . . until your partner guesses the right animal. Remember to use the Italian names of these animals!

4. You'll find more "Water Beasts" on the right-hand page. See the written names? Find the sticker that shows each animal, and put it next to its name. Can you also say and/or write its Italian name?

5. Now find the six Italian names in the puzzle. Don't forget to look in every direction, even upside down!

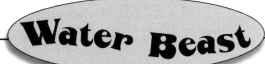

Water Beast

See Me Swim!

crocodile   shark   whale

duck   dolphin

Find Us!

pesce	T	A	R	T	A	R	U	G	A	tartaruga
	B	E	D	E	L	F	I	N	O	
balena	A	C	O	S	Q	U	A	L	O	anatra
	M	S	L	A	U	T	S	K	C	
squalo	N	E	D	W	R	C	J	T	O	delfino
	G	P	R	A	N	E	L	A	B	

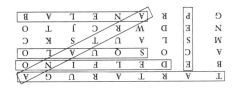 ☺

Days of the Week

Time: 45 minutes

Vocabulary and Phrases: The Seven Days of the Week

lunedì Monday • *martedì* Tuesday • *mercoledì* Wednesday • *giovedì* Thursday • *venerdì* Friday
sabato Saturday • *domenica* Sunday • *il week-end* weekend • *il giorno* day • *la settimana* week

YOU NEED ···

✔ paper
✔ a pen
✔ an old TV guide (optional)
✔ a new TV guide (optional)
✔ scissors and glue (optional)

··

1. Do you use a TV guide to decide what you're going to watch on TV? Of course you do. In "Days of the Week," you make your own TV guide!

2. To start, you need an Italian weekly calendar. So turn on the tape to learn how to say the days of the week in Italian.

3. Write the seven days of the week in Italian on a piece of paper (see the right-hand page for a model). For each day, invent the name of a TV show you'd like to watch. Say or write down that name. If you don't want to make up new shows, use the names of the TV shows you usually watch. You can also draw a clock showing the time at which each show is playing.

4. If you prefer, use an old TV guide and cut out the names and/or the illustrations of the TV shows you like. Glue them in your calendar under the day you watch that show. Be careful: Ask an adult for permission and help before you use scissors and glue.

5. Now take this week's TV guide. With the help of an adult, decide which show you will watch each day and write its name and the time it's on in your calendar. When you're finished, post your TV program in your bedroom.

6. Turn on the tape again to listen to an Italian rhyme about the seven days of the week, called *Lunedì andò da martedì* (Monday Went to Tuesday).

7. Use the calendar on the right-hand page to note the weather this week. You can draw the weather (like the sunshine), or write it down. Can you say the weather in Italian? See "Ace Inthehouse, Detective," to help you remember how. Why not note it in Italian in your calendar?

8. For each day, you can add an activity you did or note any other important information. Was it somebody's birthday? Did you get some new clothes? Try to use as much Italian as possible!

Days of the Week

Dear Daily Diary

LUNEDÌ	
MARTEDÌ	
MERCOLEDÌ	
GIOVEDÌ	
VENERDÌ	
SABATO	
DOMENICA	

Appendixes

Songs and Rhymes

MARCONDIRONDIRONDELLO

Oh! Che bel castello—
  Marcondirondirondello
Oh! Che bel castello—
  Marcondirondirondà
Il mio è ancor più bello—
  Marcondirondirondello
Il mio è ancor più bello—
  Marcondirondirondà
Noi lo ruberemo—
  Marcondirondirondello
Noi lo ruberemo—
  Marcondirondirondà
Noi lo rifaremo—
  Marcondirondirondello
Noi lo rifaremo—
  Marcondirondirondà
Noi lo bruceremo—
  Marcondirondirondello
Noi lo bruceremo—
  Marcondirondirondà
Noi lo spegneremo—
  Marcondirondirondello
Noi lo spegneremo—
  Marcondirondirondà.

CU-CÙ, CU-CÙ

L'inverno se n'è andato
La neve non c'è più
È ritornato maggio al canto del cu-cù.
Cu-cù, cu-cù,
L'inverno non c'è più
È ritornato maggio
Al canto del cu-cù.

MARCONDIRONDIRONDELLO

Oh, what a pretty castle—
  Marcondirondirondello
Oh, what a pretty castle—
  Marcondirondirondà
Mine is even prettier—
  Marcondirondirondello
Mine is even prettier—
  Marcondirondirondà
We will steal it—
  Marcondirondirondello
We will steal it—
  Marcondirondirondà
We will rebuild it—
  Marcondirondirondello
We will rebuild it—
  Marcondirondirondà
We will burn it down—
  Marcondirondirondello
We will burn it down—
  Marcondirondirondà
We will put out the fire—
  Marcondirondirondello
We will put out the fire—
  Marcondirondirondà

CUCKOO, CUCKOO

Winter is over
The snow is no longer here
May is back when the cuckoo sings
Cuckoo, cuckoo,
Winter is over
May is back
When the cuckoo sings.

La battaglia di Magenta

L'era un bel dì la battaglia di Magenta

Che bel veder cavalcare i cavalieri

Cavalieri! Al passo! Al trotto! Al galoppo!
Con una mano!
L'era una bel dì la battaglia di Magenta
Che bel veder cavalcare i cavalieri
Cavalieri! Al passo! Al trotto! Al galoppo!
Con una mano! Con due mani!
Con un piede!
L'era una bel dì la battaglia di Magenta
Che bel veder cavalcare i cavalieri
Cavalieri! Al passo! Al trotto! Al galoppo!
Con una mano! Con due mani!
Con un piede! Con due piedi!
Con la testa!

Il pollaio

Il gallo e la gallina van le oche a visitar:
"Carissime vicine siam qui per desinar
Al fuoco del tegame ci dite cosa c'è

Abbiamo tanta fame co-co co-co co-dè."
Rispondono le ochette: "Abbiamo un consommé
Di vermi e cavallette degnissime di un re

Ed una succulenta frittata si farà
A pezzi di polenta qua-qua-qua-qua-qua-qua."

E dopo aver mangiato rispose il gallo Fé:
"Andiamo in mezzo a un prato a bere un buon tè

Là ci sarà offerto dai musici di qui
Un ottimo concerto chi-chi-chi ri chi-chi."

THE BATTLE OF MAGENTA

On a fine day there was a battle in Magenta
How nice it was to watch the knights ride their horses
Knights! In step! At trot! At gallop!
With one hand!
On a fine day . . .
How nice it was . . .
Knights! In step! . . .
With one hand! With two hands!
With one foot!
On a fine day . . .
How nice it was . . .
Knights! In step! . . .
With one hand! With two hands!
With one foot! With two feet!
With your head!

THE CHICKEN PEN

The rooster and the hen visit the geese:
"Dear neighbors, we are here to eat.
Please tell us what you are cooking in the pan
We are very hungry co-co co-co co-dè."
The geese say: "We have a soup
With worms and grasshoppers that are worthy of a king
We will also make a delicious omelet
And pieces of polenta qua-qua-qua-qua-qua-qua."
After he ate, rooster Fé said:
"Let's go to a meadow and drink some tea
There the local musicians will play for us
A great concert chi-chi-chi ri chi-chi."

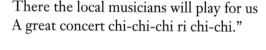

TANTI AUGURI

Tanti auguri a te,
Tanti auguri a te,
Tanti auguri a Stefano,
Tanti auguri a te!

LUNEDÌ ANDÒ DA MARTEDÌ

Lunedì andò da martedì
Per vedere se mercoledì
Avesse saputo da giovedì
Se fosse vero che venerdì
Avesse detto a sabato
Che domenica era festa.

HAPPY BIRTHDAY

Happy birthday to you,
Happy birthday to you,
Happy birthday to Stefano,
Happy birthday to you!

MONDAY WENT TO TUESDAY

Monday went to Tuesday
To find out whether Wednesday
Had been told by Thursday
Whether it was true that Friday
Had told Saturday
That Sunday was a holiday.

Glossary

Notes

All Italian words have a gender. They are either masculine or feminine. The article preceding the noun indicates the gender of the noun: *il, lo, l'* (the) and *uno, un* (a) are masculine articles; *la, l'* and *una, un'* are feminine articles. The plural masculine articles are *i, gli* and *dei, degli.* The plural feminine articles are *le* and *delle.*

• To form the plural of most nouns, simply change the final vowel to "i" for masculine nouns, and to "e" for feminine nouns. Some nouns have an irregular plural. In this glossary, irregular plurals are indicated in parentheses *(pl.)* after the singular noun.

• All adjectives agree in gender and number with the noun they modify. In this glossary, the feminine form of an adjective is indicated in parentheses *(f.)* after its masculine form.

• All words marked with an asterisk (*) are extended vocabulary not introduced in the program.

Italian–English

A

✦ AQUATIC ANIMALS ✦

l'anatra (f.)	duck
la balena	whale
*il cigno**	swan
il coccodrillo	crocodile
il delfino	dolphin
*la foca**	seal
*il pinguino**	penguin
la rana	frog
lo squalo	shark

l'anatra	duck
l'animale prediletto (m.)	pet
*l'anno**	year

B

il bagno	bathroom
la balena	whale
ballare	to dance
(io) *ballo*	I'm dancing
la banana	banana
bello (f. *bella*)	pretty, nice
fa bel tempo	it's nice (weather)
bianco (f. *bianca*)	white

✦ ✦ ✦ PETS ✦ ✦ ✦

il cane	dog
il coniglio	rabbit
il criceto	hamster
*il cucciolo**	puppy
*il gattino**	kitten
il gatto	cat
il pesce	fish
la tartaruga	turtle
l'uccello	bird

il biglietto d'auguri	card
il biscotto	cookie
blu (invariable)	blue
la bocca	mouth
(pl. *le bocche*)	
il braccio	arm
(pl. f. *le braccia*)	

✦ ✦ ✦ THE YEAR ✦ ✦ ✦

*l'anno**	year
*il mese**	month
la settimana	week
il giorno	day
*l'ora**	hour
avere	to have
(io) *ho*	I have
(io) *ho . . . anni*	I am . . . years old

buon, buono (f. *buona*)	good, happy
buon compleanno	happy birthday
buongiorno	hello

C

caldo (f. *calda*)	hot
fa caldo	it's hot (weather)

✦ ✦ ✦ AT HOME ✦ ✦ ✦

*l'armadio a muro**	closet
il bagno	bathroom
la camera da letto	bedroom
*la cantina**	cellar
*il corridoio**	hall
la cucina	kitchen
*la finestra**	window
*il garage**	garage
*la porta**	door
la sala da pranzo	dining room
il salotto	living room

la camera da letto	bedroom
la camicia	shirt

camminare	to walk
(io) *cammino*	I'm walking
la candela	candle
il cane	dog
cantare	to sing
(io) *canto*	I'm singing
i capelli	hair
il cappello	hat
la casa	house
la cassetta	tape
cattivo (f. *cattiva*)	mean
i cereali	cereals
chiamarsi	to be called
(io) *mi chiamo*	my name is
la ciliegia	cherry
cinque	five
la cioccolata	chocolate
il coccodrillo	crocodile

✦ ✦ ✦ COLORS ✦

bianco (f. *bianca*)	white
blu (invar.)	blue
giallo (f. *gialla*)	yellow
*marrone**	brown
nero (f. *nera*)	black
*rosa** (invar.)	pink
rosso (f. *rossa*)	red
verde (f. *verde*)	green
*viola** (invar.)	purple

il colore	color
il comò	chest of drawers
(pl. *i comò*)	
il compleanno	birthday
buon compleanno	happy birthday
il coniglio	rabbit
(pl. *i conigli*)	

✦ ✦ ✦ THE BODY ✦ ✦ ✦

il braccio	arm
la gamba	leg
*il ginocchio**	knee
*il gomito**	elbow
la mano	hand
la pancia	belly
il piede	foot
*la schiena**	back
*lo stomaco**	stomach
la testa	head

il corpo	body
corto (f. *corta*)	short
il criceto	hamster
la cucina	kitchen

D

il dado	die
il delfino	dolphin
dieci	ten
il divano	sofa
dodici	twelve
domenica	Sunday
due	two

E

essere	to be
(io) sono	I am
expressiones	expressions

F

fare	to do, to make
fa bel tempo/	it's nice/hot/cold
fa caldo/fa freddo	(weather)
il fiore	flower
la foto (pl. *le foto*)	photograph
la fragola	strawberry
freddo (f. *fredda*)	cold
fa freddo	it's cold
la frutta	fruit

G

la gamba	leg
il gatto	cat
gentile (f. *gentile*)	nice
la giacca	jacket
(pl. *le giacche*)	
giallo (f. *gialla*)	yellow
il giorno	day
i giorni della settimana	days of the week
giovedì	Thursday
girarsi	to turn
(io) mi giro	I'm turning

la gonna	skirt
grazie	thank you

I

in	in
nel, nella, nei, nelle	in the . . .
io	I
(io) sono	I am
(io) ho	I have
(io) ho . . . anni	I am . . . years old

L

la lampada	lamp
il letto	bed
il libro	book
lunedì	Monday
lungo (f. *lunga*)	long

M

la macedonia	fruit salad
la mano	hand
(pl. *le mani*)	
martedì	Tuesday
la maschera	mask
la mela	apple

mercoledì	Wednesday
i mobili	furniture

N

il naso	nose
nero (f. *nera*)	black
nevicare	to snow
nevica	it's snowing
no	no
nove	nine
il numero	number

O

gli occhi (m. plural.; sing. *l'occhio*)	eyes
l'orecchio (f. pl. *le orecchie*)	ear
l'orologio (pl. *gli orologi*)	watch
otto	eight

P

la palla	ball
i pantaloni	pants
la penna	pen
la pera	pear
la pesca	peach
(pl. *le pesche*)	
il pesce	fish
piangere	to cry
(io) piango	I'm crying
piccolo (f. *piccola*)	small
il piede	foot
piovere	to rain
piove	it's raining
il pirata	pirate
(pl. *i pirati*)	
la principessa	princess
il pupazzo di peluche	plush toy

Q

quattro	four

R

la rana	frog
il regalo	gift
ridere	to laugh
(io) rido	I'm laughing
rosso (f. *rossa*)	red
rotondo (f. *rotonda*)	round

S

sì	yes

sabato	Saturday	uno	one
la sala da pranzo	dining room	l'uva	grapes
il salotto	living room		
saltare	to jump	**V**	
(io) salto	I'm jumping	venerdì	Friday
il sapone	soap	verde (f. verde)	green
la scodella	bowl	il vestiti	clothes
la scrivania	desk	il vestito	dress
la sedia	chair	il viso	face
sei	six		
sette	seven		
la settimana	week		
la sorpresa	surprise		
la spazzola	(hair) brush		
lo spazzolino	toothbrush		
lo squalo	shark		
Stefano ha detto . . .	Simon says . . .		

T

la tartaruga	turtle
il tavolo	table
il telecomando	remote control

◆ ◆ ◆ THE FACE ◆ ◆ ◆

la bocca	mouth
i capelli	hair
il dente*	tooth
la guancia*	cheek
le labbra*	lips
il mento*	chin
il naso	nose
gli occhi (m.)	eyes
l'occhio	eye
l'orecchio	ear

◆ ◆ ◆ WEATHER ◆ ◆ ◆

fa bel tempo	it's nice weather
fa caldo	it's hot
fa freddo	it's cold
il fulmine*	lightning
nevica	it's snowing
la pioggia*	rain
piove	it's raining
si gela*	it's freezing
il tempo	weather
il tuono*	thunder

W

il week-end	weekend

il tempo	weather
il tesoro	treasure
la testa	head
la torta	cake

English–Italian

A

apple	la mela
aquatic animal	l'animale aquatico

◆ AQUATIC ANIMALS ◆

crocodile	il coccodrillo
dolphin	il delfino
duck	l'anatra (f.)
frog	la rana
penguin	il pinguino*
seal	la foca*
shark	lo squalo
swan	il cigno*
whale	la balena

arm	il braccio
	(pl. f. le braccia)

B

ball	la palla
banana	la banana
bathroom	il bagno
to be	essere
I am	(io) sono
I am . . .	(io) ho . . . anni
years old	
bed	il letto
bedroom	la camera da letto
bird	l'uccello
birthday	il compleanno
happy birthday	buon compleanno

◆ ◆ ◆ CLOTHES ◆ ◆ ◆

i calzini*	socks
la camicia	shirt
il cappello	hat
il cappotto*	coat
la giacca	jacket
la gonna	skirt
i jeans* (m.)	jeans
la maglietta*	T-shirt
i pantaloni	pants
il pullover*	sweater
le scarpe*	shoes
gli stivali*	boots
il vestito	dress

tre	three

U

l'uccello	bird
undici	eleven

black	nero (f. nera)
blue	blu (invar.)

◆ ◆ ◆ THE BODY

arm	il braccio
elbow	il gomito*
back	la schiena*
stomach	lo stomaco*
knee	il ginocchio*
leg	la gamba
hand	la mano
foot	il piede
head	la testa
belly	la pancia*

body	il corpo
book	il libro
bowl	la scodella
brush (hair)	la spazzola

C

cake	la torta
candle	la candela

◆ ◆ ◆ CLOTHES

boots	gli stivali
coat	il cappotto*
dress	il vestito
hat	il cappello
jacket	la giacca
jeans	i jeans* (m.)
pants	i pantaloni
shirt	la camicia
shoes	le scarpe
skirt	la gonna
socks	i calzini*
sweater	il pullover*
T-shirt	la maglietta*

card	il biglietto d'auguri
cat	il gatto
cereals	i cereali
chair	la sedia

◆ ◆ ◆ COLORS

black	nero (f. nera)
blue	blu (invar.)
brown	marrone (f. marone*)
green	verde (f. verde)
orange	arancione* (f. arancione)
pink	rosa* (invar.)
purple	viola* (invar.)
red	rosso (f. rossa)
white	bianco (f. bianca)
yellow	giallo (f. gialla)

cherry	*la ciliegia*
chest of drawers	*il comò* (pl. *i comò*)
chocolate	*la cioccolata*
clothes	*il vestiti*
cold	*freddo* (f. *fredda*)
it's cold (weather)	*fa freddo*
color	*il colore*
cookie	*il biscotto*
crocodile	*il coccodrillo*
to cry	*piangere*
I'm crying	*(io) piango*

D

to dance	*ballare*
I'm dancing	*(io) ballo*
day	*il giorno*
days of the week	*i giorni della settimana*

desk	*la scrivania*
die	*il dado*
dining room	*la sala da pranzo*
dog	*il cane*
dolphin	*il delfino*
dress	*il vestito*
duck	*l'anatra* (f.)

E

ear	*l'orecchio* (f. pl. *le orecchie*)
eight	*otto*
eleven	*undici*
expressions	*expressiones*
eyes	*gli occhi* (*l'occhio*)

✦ EXPRESSIONS ✦

Hello!	*Buongiorno!*
Good-bye!	*Arrivederci!*
See you soon!	*A presto!*
Thank you!	*Grazie!*
Happy birthday!	*Buon compleanno!*

F

face	*il viso*
fish	*il pesce*
five	*cinque*
flower	*il fiore*
foot	*il piede*
four	*quattro*

✦ THE FACE ✦

cheek	*la guancia**
chin	*il mento**
ear	*l'orecchio**
eye	*l'occhio*
eyes	*gli occhi*
hair	*i capelli*
lips	*le labbra**
mouth	*la bocca*
nose	*il naso*
tooth	*il dente**

Friday	*venerdì*
frog	*la rana*
fruit	*la frutta*

✦ FRUITS ✦

apple	*la mela*
banana	*la banana*
cherry	*la ciliegia*
grapes	*l'uva*
lemon	*il limone**
orange	*l'arancia**
peach	*la pesca*
pear	*la pera*
pineapple	*l'ananas** (m.)
plum	*la susina**
strawberry	*la fragola*

fruit salad	*la macedonia*
furniture	*i mobili*

✦ FURNITURE ✦

armchair	*la poltrona**
bed	*il letto*
bookcase	*la libreria**
chair	*la sedia*
chest of drawers	*il comò*
desk	*la scrivania*
lamp	*la lampada*
night table	*il comodino**
sofa	*il divano*
table	*il tavolo*

G

gift	*il regalo*
grapes	*l'uva*
green	*verde* (f. *verde*)

H

hair	*i capelli*
hamster	*il criceto*
hand	*la mano* (f.; pl. *le mani*)
happy	*buon, buono* (f. *buona*); *contento* (f. *contenta*)

happy birthday	*buon compleanno*
hat	*il cappello*
to have	*avere*
I have	*(io) ho*
head	*la testa*
hello	*buongiorno*
home	*la casa*

✦ AT HOME ✦

bathroom	*il bagno*
bedroom	*la camera da letto*
cellar	*la cantina**
closet	*l'armadio a muro**
dining room	*la sala da pranzo*
door	*la porta*
garage	*il garage**
hall	*il corridoio**
kitchen	*la cucina*
living room	*il salotto*
window	*la finestra**

hot	*caldo* (f. *calda*)
it's hot (weather)	*fa caldo*
house	*la casa*

I

I	*io*
I am	*(io) sono*
I am . . . years old	*(io) ho . . . anni*
in	*in*
in the	*nel, nella, nei, nelle*
it's cold/hot/nice (weather)	*fa freddo/fa caldo/ fa bel tempo*
it's raining	*piove*
it's snowing	*nevica*

J

jacket	*la giacca*
to jump	*saltare*
I'm jumping	*(io) salto*

K

kitchen	*la cucina*

L

lamp	*la lampada*
to laugh	*ridere*
I'm laughing	*(io) rido*
leg	*la gamba*
living room	*il salotto*
long	*lungo* (f. *lunga*)

M

mask	*la maschera*
mean	*cattivo* (f. *cattiva*)
Monday	*lunedì*
mouth	*la bocca* (pl. *le bocche*)
my name is	*(io) mi chiamo*

N

nice	*gentile* (f. *gentile*)

nice (weather)	*bel tempo*
it's nice weather	*fa bel tempo*
nine	*nove*
no	*no*
nose	*il naso*
number	*il numero*

✦ ✦ ✦ NUMBERS ✦ ✦ ✦

one	*uno*
two	*due*
three	*tre*
four	*quattro*
five	*cinque*
six	*sei*
seven	*sette*
eight	*otto*
nine	*nove*
ten	*dieci*
eleven	*undici*
twelve	*dodici*
twenty	*venti**
fifty	*cinquanta**
one hundred	*cento**
one thousand	*mille**
one million	*un milione**

O

one	*uno*

P

✦ ✦ ✦ PETS ✦ ✦ ✦

bird	*l'uccello*
cat	*il gatto*
dog	*il cane*
fish	*il pesce*
hamster	*il criceto*
kitten	*il gattino**
puppy	*il cucciolo**
rabbit	*il coniglio*
snake	*il serpente**
turtle	*la tartaruga*

pants	*i pantaloni*
peach	*la pesca* (pl. *le pesche*)
pear	*la pera*
pen	*la penna*
pet	*l'animale prediletto* (m.)
photograph	*la foto* (pl. *le foto*)
pirate	*il pirata* (pl. *i pirati*)
plush toy	*il pupazzo di peluche*
princess	*la principessa*

R

rabbit	*il coniglio* (pl. *i conigli*)
to rain	*piovere*
it's raining	*piove*
red	*rosso* (f. *rossa*)
remote control	*il telecomando*
round	*rotondo* (f. *rotonda*)

S

Saturday	*sabato*
seven	*sette*
shark	*lo squalo*
shirt	*la camicia*
short	*corto* (f. *corta*)
Simon says . . .	*Stefano ha detto . . .*
to sing	*cantare*
I'm singing	*(io) canto*
six	*sei*
skirt	*la gonna*
small	*piccolo* (f. *piccola*)
soap	*il sapone*
sofa	*il divano*
to snow	*nevicare*
it's snowing	*nevica*
strawberry	*la fragola*
Sunday	*domenica*
surprise	*la sorpresa*

T

table	*il tavolo*
tape	*la cassetta*
ten	*dieci*
thank you	*grazie*
three	*tre*
Thursday	*giovedì*
toothbrush	*lo spazzolino*

treasure	*il tesoro*
Tuesday	*martedì*
to turn	*girarsi*
I'm turning	*(io) mi giro*
turtle	*la tartaruga*
twelve	*dodici*
two	*due*

W

to walk	*camminare*
I'm walking	*(io) cammino*
watch	*l'orologio* (pl. *gli orologi*)
weather	*il tempo*

✦ ✦ ✦ WEATHER ✦

it's raining	*piove*
it's nice weather	*fa bel tempo*
it's hot	*fa caldo*
it's cold	*fa freddo*
it's snowing	*nevica*
it's freezing	*si gela**
thunder	*il tuono**
lightning	*il fulmine**
rain	*la pioggia**
weather	*il tempo**

Wednesday	*mercoledì*
week	*la settimana*
weekend	*il week-end*
whale	*la balena*
white	*bianco* (f. *bianca*)

Y

year	*l'anno*

✦ ✦ ✦ THE YEAR ✦

year	*l'anno**
month	*il mese**
week	*la settimana*
day	*il giorno*
hour	*l'ora**

yellow	*giallo* (f. *gialla*)
yes	*sì*

LA CASSETTA

LA PENNA

LA FOTO

IL DADO

L'OROLOGIO

BUON

COMPLEANNO